AF592877

SOUTHERN STEAM LOCOMOTIVE SURVEY

in the Southern Steam series

Southern Steam Locomotive Survey: Maunsell Early Classes
Southern Steam Locomotive Survey: Maunsell Later Classes
Southern Steam Locomotive Survey: Bulleid Merchant Navy Pacifics
Southern Steam Locomotive Survey: Bulleid West Country Pacifics
Southern Steam Locomotive Survey: Urie Classes
Southern Steam Locomotive Survey: Drummond Classes
Southern Steam Locomotive Survey: Adams Classes
Southern Steam in Action: 1
Southern Steam in Action: 2
Southern Steam in Action: 3
Southern Steam on Shed
More Southern Steam on Shed
Southern Steam from Lineside
Southern Steam—South and East
More Southern Steam—South and East
Southern Steam—South and West
More Southern Steam—South and West
Southern Steam on the Isle of Wight
Steam on the Brighton Line
Southern Steam in the West Country
More Southern Steam in the West Country
Southern Steam in Close-up
Southern Steam—Preserved
Southern Steam—Doubleheaded
Southern Steam Branch Lines
Southern Steam 1923–39

SOUTHERN STEAM LOCOMOTIVE SURVEY

THE EARLY MAUNSELL CLASSES

edited by Tony Fairclough & Alan Wills

D. BRADFORD BARTON LTD

ISBN 0 85153 243 8

printed in Great Britain by Chapel River Press (IPC Printers), Andover
for the publishers

D. BRADFORD BARTON LTD · Trethellan House · Truro · Cornwall · England

introduction

Of the four Companies formed at the Railway Grouping of 1923, only the Great Western could proceed with its locomotive development in an orderly manner unhindered by the shotgun marriages of unlikely bedfellows which bedevilled the other three Companies. Of the Southern's main constituents, the LSWR was the most powerful, but its well-loved Chief Mechanical Engineer, Robert Urie, was of an age for retirement. The Directors offered the position to the next in line, Richard Maunsell, CME of the SECR at Ashford, and the subsequent history of Southern locomotive development in the following years was to prove the wisdom of their choice. Maunsell had the difficult task of welding together the three very different traditions eminating from Ashford, Eastleigh and Brighton and it is to his credit that he very largely succeeded. However, the practices of Ashford and Eastleigh could clearly be discerned in Maunsell's locomotives and it was not until the arrival of the mercurial Bulleid in 1937 that the last vestiges of former days were swept away. Maunsell's work in this field parallels that of his great contemporary Sir Nigel Gresley on the LNER and both of these engineers can take much credit for avoiding in their respective companies the situation which hampered progress on the LMS in its early years.

While Maunsell was not a great innovating engineer in the Churchward or Chapelon mould, he had the very valuable attribute of being able to evaluate accurately the work of others and to integrate new ideas into practical locomotive designs so that his engines combined the best features of current thinking. Furthermore, on his appointment at Ashford in 1913 he had been able to gather together highly qualified staff to design and build the locomotives he had in mind. Among these, G. H. Pearson (Assistant CME and Works Manager, Ashford) and H. Holcroft (Works Assistant, and an expert on valve gears and valve setting) came from Swindon with their knowledge of Churchward's latest practices, while J. Clayton (Chief Draughtsman) was recruited from Derby and brought with him the Midland Railway's penchant for beauty and symmetry in locomotive design. When the Southern's central design section was established at Waterloo in 1923, Clayton and Holcroft were appointed as assistants to the CME and so the team continued to work together for the enlarged system.

As an example of Maunsell's ability to absorb the best in British locomotive practice, his 'N' Class Mogul can be considered. Here was a machine which for the first time combined much of the high-pressure boiler design and the long-travel valve theory of Swindon with the additional vital ingredient of superheating, plus the ease of servicing and maintenance associated with two outside cylinders and Walschaerts valve gear. Of course, Chapelon's dramatic work on steam passage design was yet to come, as were such labour-saving features as rocking grates and self-cleaning smokeboxes, but the 'N' Class 2-6-0 can be seen as a thoroughly modern locomotive, yet dating from as long ago as 1917. Unlike many other Chiefs who preferred to disparage the work of their predecessors, Maunsell could assess the good qualities of existing locomotives with a view to improving their basic design with his own ideas, the prime example being his 'King Arthur' 4-6-0s which were modifications of the Urie 'N15' Class from the LSWR.

Once the initial problems of Grouping had been overcome and sufficient 'King Arthurs' and mixed-traffic 4-6-0s and 2-6-0s were on the road, the CME was then able to give his attention to completely new designs. However, the story of the 'Lord Nelsons', 'Schools' and other later classes will be dealt with in a further volume as this one deals largely with the classes which were developed from pre-Grouping designs, with the addition of the 'Z' 0-8-0T of 1929 (which had a Brighton boiler).

While the success or otherwise of locomotive designs can be assessed from many angles—low capital cost, fuel economy, ease of maintenance, reliability, etc.—nevertheless the grass-roots opinion of the men who had to work on them day in and day out can be as good a guide as any and there is no doubt that all the classes depicted in this study were very popular with the men. Their quality may be summarised by the Salisbury driver who, having to work a regular express duty over 'foreign' metals to Cardiff using Western 4-6-0s, longed 'to see what a good 'King Arthur' or 'Black-un' could do on the job'. Such confidence tells its own story.

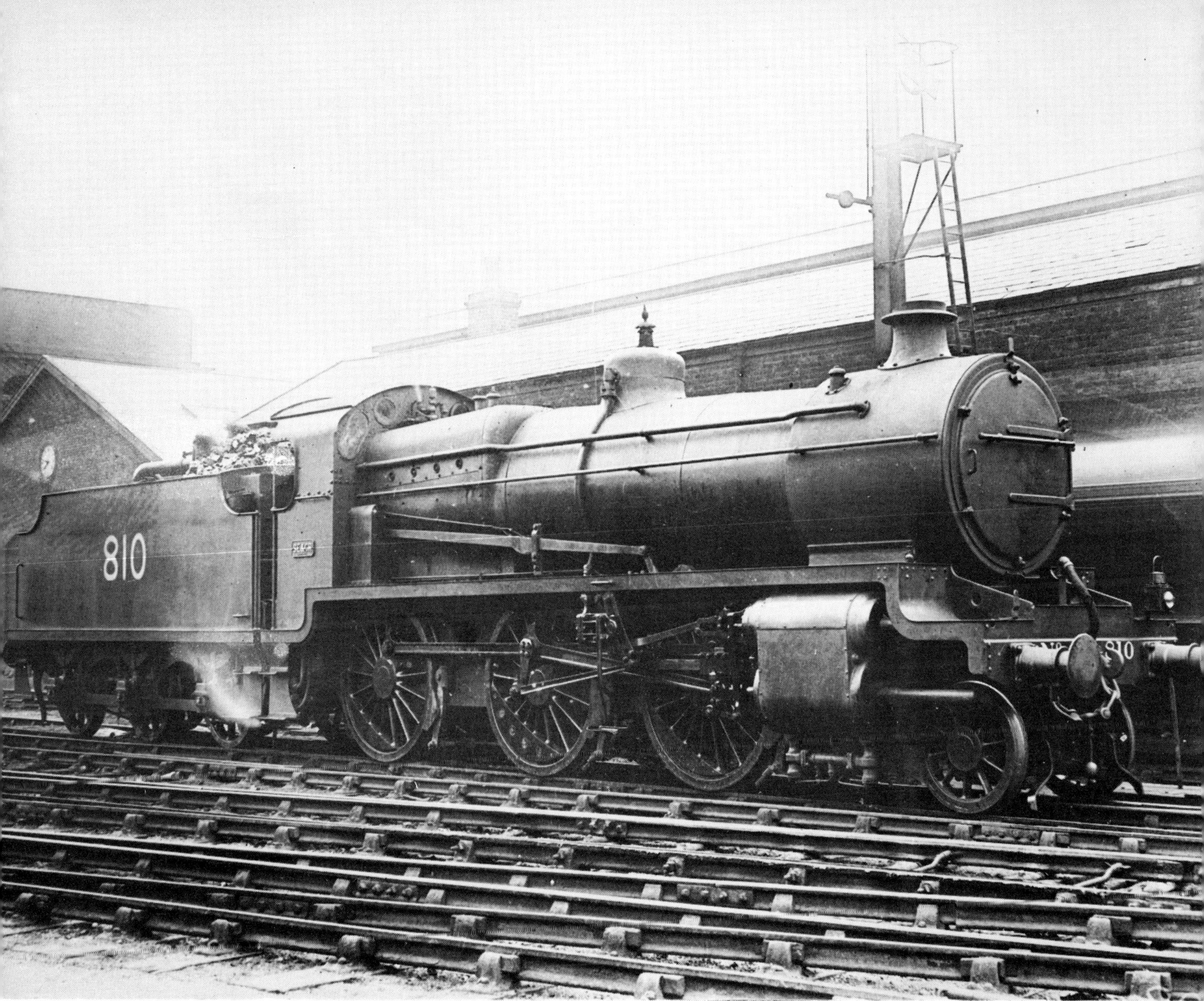

The pioneer 'N' Class 2-6-0, SECR No.810, at Bricklayers Arms on 25 May 1920. When this locomotive appeared from Ashford Works in 1917 it had the distinction of being the most advanced design in the country. Such features as the high boiler pressure (200lb per sq.in) and long-travel piston valves followed Churchward practice on the GWR, but the provision of high superheat was a Maunsell addition to the formula of success. [L. T. George collection]

Following the ten SECR-built 'N' Class 2-6-0s, the Southern Railway purchased 50 more which had been built to Government orders at Woolwich Arsenal in the mid-1920's. From this circumstance derived the nickname of the class—'Woolworths'. Many of the new machines were drafted to Exmouth Junction shed for use west of Exeter, where they became an immediate success. No. 1829 is seen on the turntable at Ilfracombe soon after its construction. [Aubrey Parminter]

One of the newly-built 'N' Class Moguls, No.837, brings its train to a halt at Bere Alston on 14 June 1926. These modern machines became extremely popular with the men who had to work them on the steeply graded lines in Devon and Cornwall, and in the pre-war years were excellently maintained by the staff at Exmouth Junction shed. [H. C. Casserley]

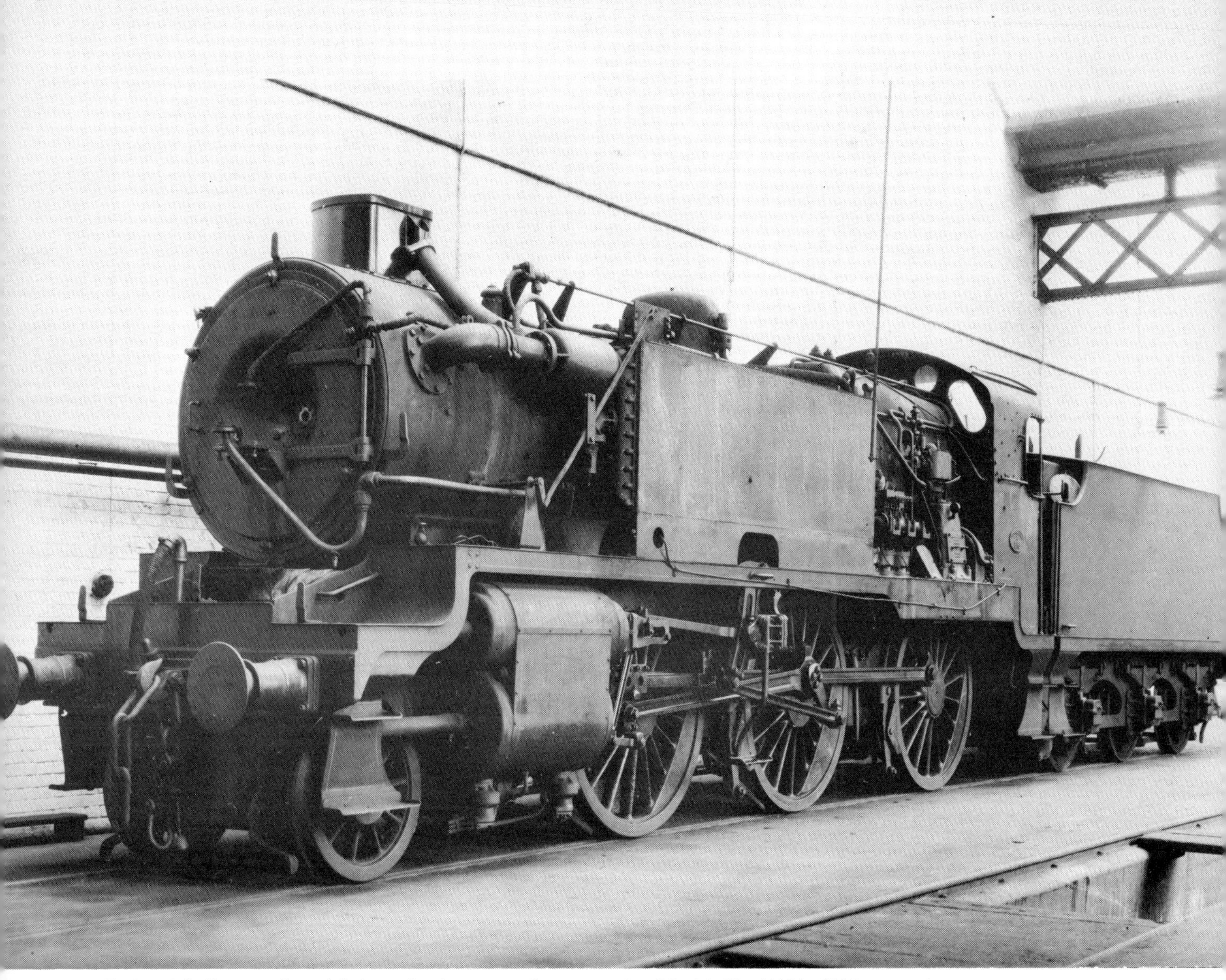

Fortunately the experimental steam heat conservation apparatus fitted to No.1816 in 1932 was not a success otherwise all the 'Woolworths' might have had their handsome good-looks disfigured in this way! All the exhaust steam was returned to the boiler and the draught for the fire was obtained by means of a fan.
[L. T. George collection]

A 'Woolworth' in typical 1930's guise. No.1836, seen at Cowley Bridge Junction, near Exeter, in 1937, ha had smoke deflectors added, and the piston tail-rods removed. The 'Midland' influence among Maunsell' design staff can be discerned in such features as the chimney, cab profile and tender design, all of whic have been carefully styled. [Gattey Windeatt

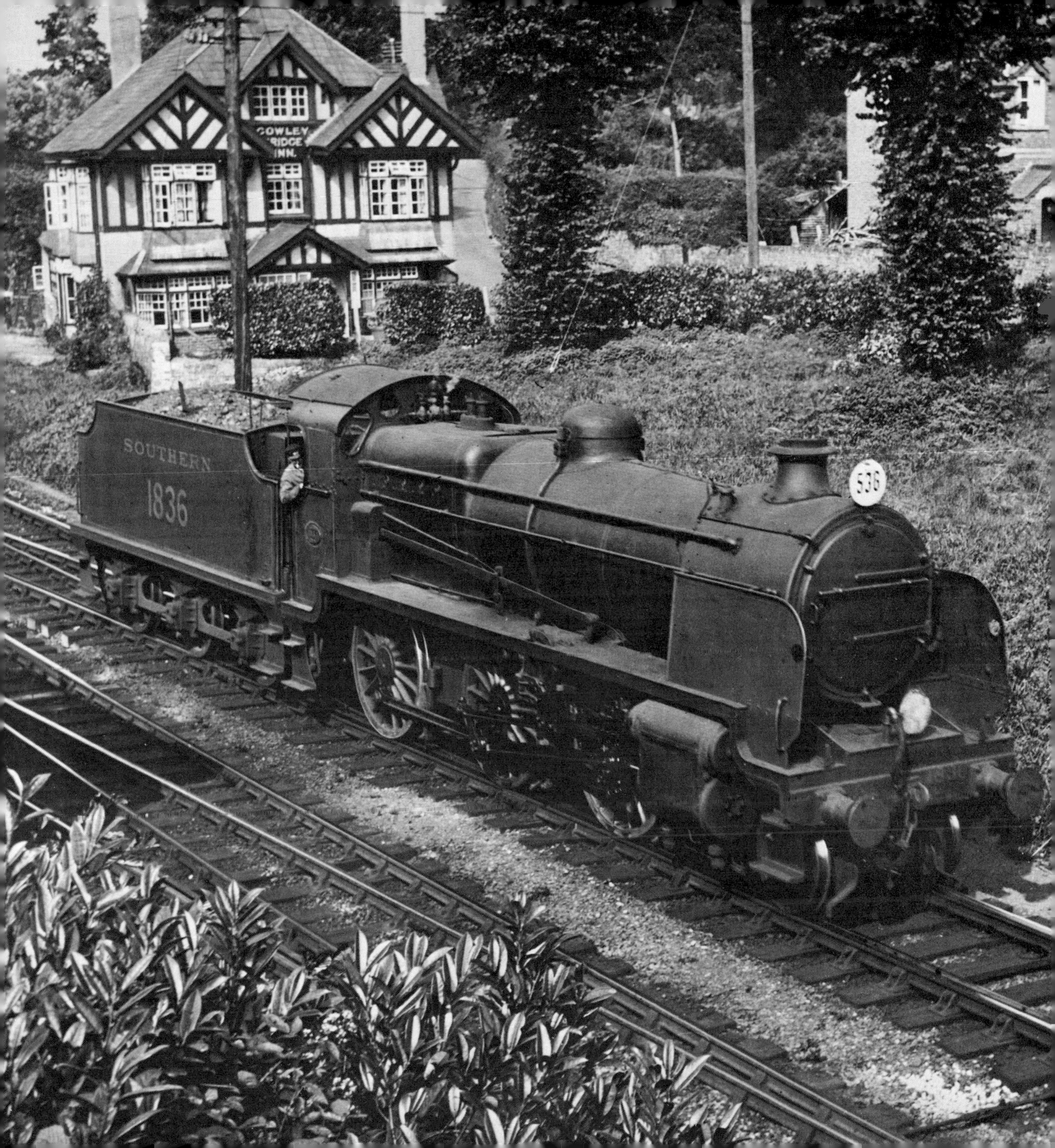
COWLEY
INN.
SOUTHERN
1836
536

No.31816 again, this time towards the end of its long career. The engine had long since lost its snifting valves from the smokebox and had acquired a later Maunsell style chimney when it was seen hurrying away from Dorking on its old SECR metals with a Redhill to Reading train on 3 January 1965, during the last week of steam working in this service. [G. D. King]

No.31872, which has been fitted with a Standard-type chimney, has a heavy load on the 5.25 p.m. London Bridge t Reading South on a summer evening in 1961. The engine is hard at work near Purley Oaks. [D. T. Cobbe

With the regulator shut and steam pressure rising, No.31864 is pushed by its load down the 1 in 200 ban towards Dorking in September 1957. These 5ft 6in Moguls performed a great deal of freight work around th Home Counties throughout their existence. [A. R. Butche

31872
31864

A dramatic photograph of No.31825 leaving the snow-covered Tonbridge West Yard with a freight on 26 April 1950. [J. E. Turley]

A lengthy Guildford–Reading parcels train rumbles along near Ash Junction behind No.31817 in 1962. [G. D. King]

'Woolworths' were often rostered to work the heavy stone trains, both from the quarry at Meldon, near Okehampton, and in the London area. Once the heavy stone hoppers were on the move, these ballast trains could proceed at a good speed because they were vacuum-braked and so could easily be brought to a halt. No.31862, heading for Tonbridge, was photographed on 27 April 1954. [R. K. Taylor]

With road traffic hindered by the inclement weather, 'Woolworth' No.31869 suffers little inconvenience as it presses on towards Reading from the rural Betchworth station on 16 March 1964. The coaches are special narrow Hastings line stock made redundant by the introduction of the diesel-electric multiple units in the mid-1950's. [G. D. King]

Most Maunsell Moguls were sent to Ashford for shopping until the Works closed. On 14 October 1961, No.31839 of Exmouth Junction (72A) looks spick and span after its visit to Ashford, and has been rostered to the 4.10 p.m. Tonbridge to Eastbourne while it remains in the South East. [D. T. Cobbe]

No.31827 had unusually been coupled to a wider 4,000 gallon Maunsell tender (possibly from a withdrawn 'Schools') when it was seen at Dorking (Town) on 11 April 1964. [A. R. Butcher]

Guildford's No.31811 looks clean and steam-tight as it leaves Betchworth on a bright sunny autumn afternoon in October 1964. Because these engines often worked passenger trains they were painted lined black by British Railways, a livery which suited the design quite well. [G. D. King]

No. 31862 also had a 4,000 gallon tender by 1965. The Mogul was working on the Reading–Redhill services during the last few days of steam working, in January 1965. [G. D. King]

'N' Class Mogul No.31868 receives attention to the valves inside Redhill shed, January 1962. These Maunsell engines were among the first in Britain which could be prepared by their drivers without having to stand over a pit. The idea of easily accessible oiling points was something new in 1917. [A. R. Butcher]

'Woolworths' were to be found throughout the Southern system. No.31816 stands outside its home shed, Eastleigh, on 23 June 1963. In common with most of the SR's main-line locomotives, the Mogul has been fitted with AWS equipment beneath the buffer beam. [D. M. Cox]

No. 31852 in Eastleigh Works.
[Lens of Sutton]

No.31859, undergoing what was probably its last general overhaul in the erecting shop at Eastleigh Works, 21 April 1963. The 19in diameter piston is prominent in the foreground. What would seem to be a steam dome in front of the Belpaire firebox is in reality top-feed apparatus, the boiler design in fact being reminiscent of Great Western practice. [D. M. Cox]

The lush foliage of the New Forest forms a scenic backdrop for No.31866 as it works a down local near Brockenhurst Junction on 24 August 1963. [D. M. Cox]

No. 31824, the last of the SECR-constructed 'N's, still at work on its home metals, at Chislehurst, on 15 April 1957. At the time this was one of sixteen 'N' Class 2-6-0s at Bricklayers Arms (73B) for working freights between London and the Kent Coast towns.
[A. R. Butcher]

31824

ANDOVER
31873
31816

One of Exmouth Junction's (Exeter) large stud of 'N's saunters up the main line near Sidmouth Junction with a permanent way train on 2 August 1961. [M. J. Fox]

Although many newer Standard classes were available, the Maunsell Moguls continued to work a number of stopping trains in Hampshire and Wiltshire until 1965. No.31873 accelerates away from Andover Junction with the 10.24 a.m. Basingstoke to Salisbury on 12 March 1965. [D. T. Cobbe]

The fireman has time for a rest on his seat as No.31816 rolls along near Lymington Junction with the 11.53 a.m. Eastleigh to Bournemouth stopper, 2 September 1961. [D. T. Cobbe]

No.31875, working the 11.25 a.m. goods on 16 May 1963, has pulled over on to the down road at Otterham to allow the 1.12 p.m. from Wadebridge to overtake. [J. R. Besley]

'Woolworths' remained associated with the lines west of Exeter for 40 years. The signalman at Wadebridge holds out the tablet for the section to St. Kew Highway as No. 31830 with the 11.25 a.m. goods to Exmouth Junction pulls away from the Cornish market town, 14 July 1951.
[Brian A. Butt]

A freight from Exmouth Junction yard winds down the grade towards Bere Ferrers on the Plymouth road, behind No. 31851 on 20 April 1954. The 'N' 2-6-0s handled the majority of such freights on the lines west of Exeter, a task for which they were ideally suited. They were preferred to the more powerful 'West Country' Pacifics because of their greater braking capability—a freight locomotive's loading being determined by its ability to stop a given tonnage rather than pulling it.
[Brian A. Butt]

It is perhaps appropriate to complete this section dealing with the 'N' Class 2-6-0 with views of the engines at work in the West of England. Although supplanted by the Bulleid Pacifics on many duties, and assisted by 'T9s' and the later Standard locomotives, nevertheless the 'Woolworths' seemed to form the backbone of the locomotive stud on these routes. No. 31845 is seen, hard at work near Coleford Junction with the Ilfracombe portion of the 'Atlantic Coast Express' on 23 March 1963. [W. L. Underhay]

Exmouth Junction shed usually had about 25 'N's on its strength, and full use was made of their 26,035lb of tractive effort on all classes of duty. In poor condition externally yet steaming well, No.31855 slows down for the curves at Cowley Bridge Junction, where the SR and WR meet near Exeter, as it hauls the 2.10 p.m. Ilfracombe to Waterloo on 11 August 1962. Another fifteen 'N's, Nos.1400–1414 were built in the early 1930's and will be discussed in a later volume.
[W. L. Underhay]

Until 1925, only 4-4-0s were permitted on the Chatham line between Victoria and Chislehurst. Maunsell took eleven of the Wainwright 'E' Class 4-4-0s and rebuilt them completely. First, SECR No.179 was converted at Ashford, then the remaining ten were dealt with by Beyer Peacock Ltd at Gorton. No.31067 works a special from Eastleigh on 22 May 1960.
[A. E. Bennett]

The 'E1's could haul 300-ton boat trains over the Dover road with ease. Although supplanted by the large types made available after Grouping, they continued to perform excellently. No.31497 of Bricklayers Arm has full steam up prior to working a parcels train out of London Bridge on 6 July 1951. [Brian Morrisor

31497
91

Following the great success of the 'E1's, Maunsell rebuilt twenty 'D' Class 4-4-0s to 'D1' specifications in 1921. Very similar to the 'E1's in appearance, the 'D1's could be distinguished by their plain, instead of fluted, coupling rods. This view of 'D1' No.31739 shows the 4-4-0 leaving Chevening, working the 2.50 p.m. Dunton Green to Westerham on 28 October 1961, the last day of working on the branch. [D. T. Cobbe]

No. 31749 prepares to come off shed at Stewarts Lane shortly after Nationalisation. The 6ft 8in driving wheels, allied to long travel valves actuated by Stephenson valve gear, made these engines exceptionally free-running, and the hard-driving men at 'The Lane' performed wonders with them. [Peter Winding]

'D1' No.31739 and 'E1' No.31067 stand together on shed at Tonbridge, 28 May 1961. The similarity of the two rebuilds is clearly apparent, while the family likeness to the 'Woolworths' can also be discerned. [D. T. Cobbe]

An 'E1' 4-4-0 unusually seen on freight work, but as the hoppers are vacuum-braked, the brake power o No.31019 will be capable of stopping the ballast-laden train. The scene is Paddock Wood on Saturda 22 April 1961. [D. T. Cobbe

Another 'D1'/'E1' combination, Nos. 31749 and 31067 respectively, both cleaned up for working a special on 4 November 1961. The 'E1' has 6ft 6in wheels, but the class were just as speedy as the 'D1's. Both engines have 180lb per sq.in. superheated boilers with Belpaire fireboxes. [D. T. Cobbe]

'D1' No. 31749 again, this time seen in Ashford Works in September 1960 receiving a general overhaul. It's companion is ex-LBSCR 'C2X' 0-6-0 No. 32449. [M. Jackson]

No. 31735 works another typical 'D1' turn—the 6.36 p.m. Maidstone (West) to Charing Cross—near Hildenborough on 2 August 1954. [R. K. Taylor

No. 31749 yet again, this time in action shortly before its entry into the Works as pictured previously. The 4-4-0 swings into Sevenoaks in July 1960 with the 7.24 p.m. Holborn Viaduct to Dover. [G. D. King]

'D1' No.31505 hauls its Maunsell stock away from Faversham *en route* to Canterbury on 12 July 1952. It will be noted that these Maunsell 4-4-0s did not have the top feed apparatus as did the various designs of Moguls. [P. J. Lynch]

263
171
31505
31505

When further medium powered passenger engines were required in the South East, Maunsell introduced his 'L1' 4-4-0 design in 1926. These were an updated version of the Wainwright 'L' 4-4-0 of 1914. No.31756 is working the 11.38 a.m. Tonbridge to Reading near Tonbridge, 27 April 1954.
[R. K. Taylor]

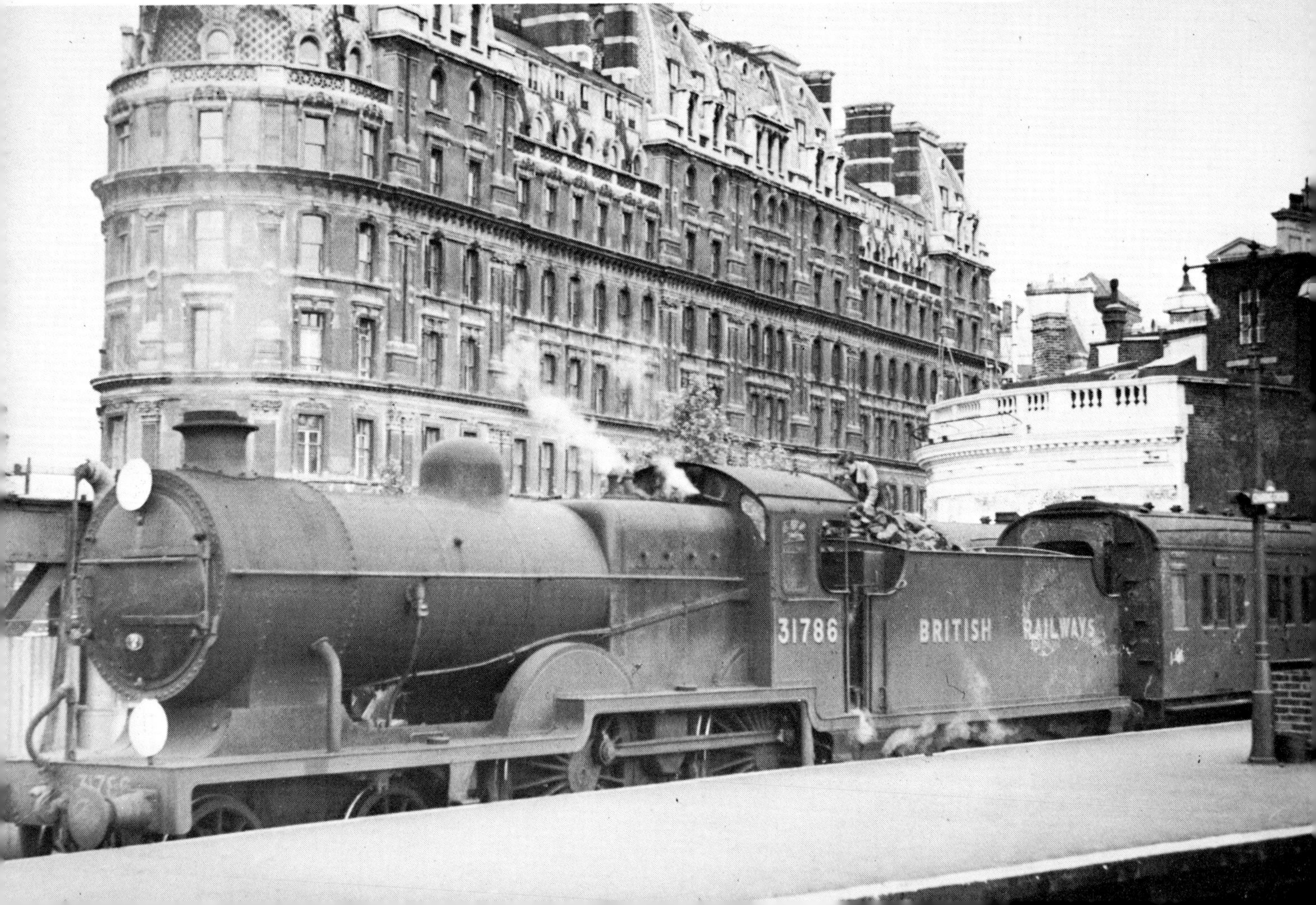

'L1' No. 31756 of Ashford shed heads away from its home town with an up train on 22 May 1954. These 4-4-0s, with long-travel valves were speedy runners, and could be distinguished from the 'D1's and 'E1's by the later design of chimney, side-window cab and the Maunsell flat-sided six-wheeled tender. The twenty engines were built by the North British Locomotive Company of Glasgow and spent much of their life on the London–Hastings and London–Folkestone and Deal lines. [Brian Morrison]

No. 31786, in early BR livery, prepares to leave Charing Cross for the Kent coast on 5 July 1951. The general dimensions were similar to the 'D1's, the driving wheels being 6ft 8in, the cylinders half inch larger diameter at $19\frac{1}{2}$in $\times$ 36in and the boiler pressure 180lb per sq.in. [Brian Morrison]

The prototype 'N1' No.31822 steams slowly westward on the long straight stretch between Ashford and Tonbridge with coal empties on 16 April 1958. At that time the 'N1's were all shedded at Hither Green.
[A. R. Butcher]

In 1922, Maunsell built SECR No.822 as a 3-cylinder version of the 'N' Mogul design. The valves of the 16in × 28in cylinders were actuated by a conjugated valve gear designed by H. Holcroft, a rocking lever system operating the middle valve from the outside gears. No.1876 was one of five further 'N1's which were built (with three sets of valve gear) in 1930.
[L. T. George collection]

The 11.20 a.m. Hither Green to Paddock Wood freight drifts out of Polhill Tunnel behind No. 31822 on 13 April 1954.
[R. K. Taylor]

'N1' No.31880, now of Tonbridge shed, is hard at work near Sandling in 1958. As the three-cylinder Moguls had a lighter hammer blow on the track than their two cylinder companions, they were popular with the Civil Engineer and although more economical on fuel, their steaming was none too good at times so they could not be pressed as hard as the standard 'Woolworths'. [D. T. Cobbe]

No. 31822 again, in company with 'N' Class 2-6-0 No. 31856 at Gravesend on 20 June 1952. The three-cylinder 'N1's and 'U1's differed from the two-cylinder designs at the front end. The running plates were carried straight out to the front of the locomotive and then dropped straight down to the buffer beam, giving these designs their distinctive appearance. The smoke deflectors were of a special short design to match the running plates. [Brian Morrison]

Maunsell's first express design for the SR, No. 453 *King Arthur*, poses for an official photograph, (taken with a wide-angle lens?) at Waterloo early in 1925. Although brand-new engines, the Nos. 448–457 series were coupled to redundant Drummond tenders taken from the withdrawn 4-6-0s bearing the same numbers. These tenders were retained in service until the mid 1950's. [Peter Winding collection]

As the size of locomotive boilers increased, problems occurred with drifting exhaust steam obscuring the driver's view from the cab. At first, engineers believed that sharpening the blast would help, but, following Continental practice, it was discovered that deflector plates would reduce the problem. An early clumsy-looking experimental design is seen on No. 772 *Sir Percivale*, pictured c.1930 at Waterloo, where the old gantry signal box is in evidence. During 1930, No. 772 was transferred to Stewarts Lane and received a six-wheeled tender. The driver is giving his regular engine that extra drop of oil which is symbolic of the care which drivers lavished on 'their' engines. [Peter Winding collection]

Because express engines were urgently required, an order for thirty 'King Arthurs' was placed with the North British Locomotive Company in January 1925, and the first deliveries began in May of that year. Costing £10,085 each, these engines had the modified Maunsell cab which would fit the restricted Eastern Section loading gauge, and were coupled to 5,000 gallon Urie-type tenders. No. 778 *Sir Pelleas,* seen at Nine Elms, came south from Glasgow in June 1925. [Peter Winding collection]

When Maunsell took command as CME of the newly formed Southern Railway in 1923 he realised that the Urie 'N15' 4-6-0 was a fine express design, and that with a few modifications could be the basis of an excellent express locomotive. The general layout of the frames, boiler and firebox was the same, but the modified engines belonged to the 'Churchward era', having higher boiler pressure, an enlarged superheater and long-travel valves. This view, taken on the pits at Nine Elms, 19 September 1925, shows one of the original Urie engines, No. 746, in the foreground, while behind it is one of the Maunsell version, No. 774 *Sir Gaheris*.
[H. C. Casserley]

Nº 46

After running its trials, No. 453 *King Arthur* went to Salisbury shed, where it remained until withdrawal in July 1961. During the halcyon days before the Second World War it was a regular engine in Salisbury's Top Link (along with Nos. 454/5/7). When photographed near Chard Junction with the 12.36 p.m. from Salisbury on 19 April 1939, it was driven, turn and turn about, by Drivers Witt and Cann and no doubt it is one of these stalwarts who is just visible on the footplate. Few of the excellent lumps of coal on the tender will be burnt on this easy down trip, but most will disappear when working the heavy 5.55 p.m. up from Exeter in the evening. [L. T. George collection]

A close-up of No. 457 *Sir Bedivere* on the Works Line at Eastleigh shed, 3 June 1934. The big 4-6-0 is waiting to go into the nearby shops for a general overhaul, probably having completed some 50,000 miles of express running since its last visit. In those days, Top Link engines were maintained in superb mechanical condition. Their regular drivers booked every small defect they could find and in a hard water area like Salisbury they were washed out every seven days. Among the men associated with this engine were Drivers Thorner and Williams. [L. T. George collection]

The 'King Arthurs' often worked in the same Link as the bigger and more powerful 'Lord Nelsons' at Nine Elms shed in the 1930's, and were by no means out-classed. No. 773 *Sir Lavaine* takes the curve at Worting Junction with the down 'Bournemouth Belle' in 1937. [L. T. George collection]

The thirty Glasgow-built 'Arthurs' were usually known as the 'Scotsmen'. No.777 *Sir Lamiel* was reputedly the best of them all. In the pre-war years it was usually at Nine Elms but the engine had several spells of allocation to the Eastern Section, and was shedded at Ramsgate in 1937, when photographed here at Dover. No.777's greatest exploit was the classic 1936 run with Driver Alderman of Nine Elms at the regulator when the 83 miles from Salisbury to Waterloo were reeled off in 72 minutes—with 345 tons behind the tender. It is indeed fortunate that *Sir Lamiel* has been preserved for posterity. [D. T. Cobbe]

No.783 *Sir Gillemere* of Bournemouth has an easy run down to Weymouth with a local train on 8 July 1935. The setting is near Moreton, five miles east of Dorchester. [L. T. George collection]

No. 766 *Sir Geraint* works a Bournemouth express past Woking, 16 September 1946.
[Brian A. Butt]

Bulleid's successful modifications to the 'Nelson' blastpipes were followed by the fitting of a Lemaitre blast pipe and wide diameter chimney to No. 792 *Sir Hervis de Revel* in 1940. Unfortunately the modifications did not result in the desired improvement and eventually in 1952, the engine reverted to standard. Allocated new to Bournemouth, No. 792 went to Exmouth Junction in 1937 and then had moved on to Nine Elms by 1949 when it was seen at West Byfleet on 20 May with a down stopper. [D. T. Cobbe]

Following its initial allocation to Bournemouth, No. 789 *Sir Guy* moved to Exmouth Junction, among the Nos. 786–792 series, in the general reshuffle of 1937. The immaculate 4-6-0 is seen breasting Hewish summit with the up 'Atlantic Coast Express' on 19 April 1939. At that time, Bulleid was experimenting with various liveries, and *Sir Guy* looks smart in its unique light green and black paintwork. [L. T. George collection]

'King Arthur' Class Nos. 793–806 were built at Eastleigh Works in 1926 and were fitted with Maunsell 3500 gallon six-wheeled tenders for use on the Central Section. Following the electrification of the Brighton routes in 1933, these 4-6-0s were transferred to the Eastern Section, where they performed until the late 1950s. No. 804 *Sir Cador of Cornwall* is seen in post-war malachite green livery. [L. T. George collection]

The nameplate of No 804
Sir Cador of Cornwall
[D. H. Ballantyne]

No. 800 *Sir Meleaus de Lile* stands in the yard at Eastleigh shed following a visit to the shops, 10 March 1935. The snifting valves on the smokebox were removed in later years. [L. T. George collection]

Bricklayers Arms cleaners had worked hard on No. 798 *Sir Hectimere* before it powered the 9.15 a.m. Charing Cross to Ramsgate on 9 April 1948. The train is seen between Sandling and Shorncliffe. [D. T. Cobbe]

No. 451 *Sir Lamorak* is covered in war-time grime as it heads the milk empties westwards near Templecombe on 11 May 1945. From 1942 to 1946, unlined black was the standard SR livery, a finish which did little justice to the splendid lines of 'King Arthurs'. [L. T. George collection]

The 'King Arthurs' spent much of the war hauling heavy freight trains, and in the post-war years, following the introduction of the Pacifics to the best turns, they were often to be seen on such duties as this goods hauled by No. 30451 *Sir Lamorak* at Salisbury on 2 July 1954. [Brian Morrison]

No. 30457 *Sir Bedivere* on Eastern Region territory at Neasden with a transfer freight, 5 July 1952. [Brian Morrison]

30451
30457

Although photographed after Nationalisation (2 October 1948), No. 769 *Sir Balan* still retains the Bulleid malachite green livery which suited the 'Scotsmen' very well. The Stewarts Lane engine is passing Cheriton Junction, with the 2.50 p.m. boat train from Folkestone Harbour to Victoria. [D. T. Cobbe]

Following the widespread introduction of the Bulleid light Pacifics to the West of England, the 'King Arthurs' were drafted away from Exmouth Junction shed to perform duties in the Home Counties. No. 30789 *Sir Guy* races through Walton-on-Thames on the 'down main' with the 10.54 a.m. Waterloo to Salisbury in September 1949. Note the LSWR lower quadrant signals which were still in use at the time. [D. T. Cobbe]

Before a standard livery was adopted by British Railways, engines continued to be turned out in their old colours. No. 30456 *Sir Galahad,* ex-Works at Eastleigh on 23 October 1948, is lettered in the temporary style of Gill Sans lettering used by the Southern during this period. [John H. Meredith]

271
BRITISH RAILWAYS
30456

No. 30453 *King Arthur* remained a fine engine to the end. The *doyen* of the class is seen speeding through Raynes Park on a typical Salisbury 'King Arthur' turn of the post-war years, the 8.43 a.m. semi-fast from Salisbury to Waterloo, 29 May 1956. The 4,300 gallon Drummond tenders were a great handicap on the non-stop 83 mile run between Salisbury and Waterloo, but the crew could 'top-up' at Andover Junction or Basingstoke on duties such as this. In later years, Nos. 30448–57 acquired 5000 gallon Urie tenders from withdrawn Urie 'N15's, which relieved the anxieties of the footplatemen considerably.
[A. R. Butcher]

30453

During the early post-war years, the Eastern Section 'King Arthurs' settled down to their usual task of hauling express and semi-fast commuter trains between the dormitory towns of Kent and the capital. No.30804 *Sir Cador of Cornwall* draws into Sevenoaks with an early morning train to London Bridge on 16 April 1958. [A. R. Butcher]

Sunlight and shadow at Cannon Street, 25 April 1951. The fireman of No.30806 *Sir Galleron*, the last of t
'Arthurs' to be built, has coupled up ready for a run down to the coast. [Brian Morris

182
30806

No. 30800 *Sir Meleaus de Lile,* shedded at Bricklayers Arms (73B), approaching Folkestone Junction with empty coaching stock from Dover Marine in 1955. The number 101 on the disc is the locomotive duty roster number, the 127 on the smokebox is the Operating Department's train number. [D. T. Cobbe]

No. 30800, again at Folkestone Junction, 16 July 1955, at the head of a rake of ex-SECR 'birdcage' stock. Somehow, to those used to the Western Section 'Arthurs', the six-wheeled tender seemed much too small to suit the rugged lines of the heavy 4-6-0.
[D. T. Cobbe]

Following the spread of electrification in Kent, the Eastern Section 'King Arthurs' gradually migrated westwards. No. 30794 *Sir Ector de Maris* now of Eastleigh shed, heads a Southampton to Waterloo semi-fast near Weybridge in July 1959. The 3,500 gallon tenders caused problems on the longer Western Section runs, and eventually the drawgear and rear framing of some of these 'Arthurs' were altered to allow the large 5,000 gallon tenders to be coupled. However No. 30794 retained its six-wheeler to the end. [Derek Cross]

At a time when the Bulleids hauled the majority of the top turns, it was pleasant to see the 'Kentish Belle' Pullman express rocketing along behind 4-6-0 No. 30767 *Sir Valence* on 19 August 1958. The express has just come off the Chislehurst loop with its eight heavy luxury cars. [A. R. Butcher]

The nameplate of No. 30793 *Sir Ontzlake*. [C. E. Dann]

After spending many years on the Eastern Section, the original 'Scotsman', No. 30763 *Sir Bors de Ganis* moved to Eastleigh in the mid-fifties, where, with nine companions it worked boat trains and semi-fasts between Southampton and Waterloo. On 17 April 1957, it was seen heading the 10.54 a.m. Waterloo to Salisbury stopper, Eastleigh duty No. 251, which involved this turn down the Salisbury line, returning with the 4.5 p.m. Salisbury to Waterloo slow. [A. R. Butcher]

251

Basingstoke shed always seemed to acquire other depots' cast-offs for its semi-fast duties to Waterloo. No. 30456 *Sir Galahad* had come from Salisbury and is seen passing Raynes Park with the 3.54 p.m. Waterloo to Basingstoke on 7 September 1957. This engine received the Urie 5,000 gallon tender from condemned No. 30749 in August 1958. [P. J. Lynch]

The up 'Union Castle Express' thunders through Surbiton behind Eastleigh 4-6-0 No. 30770 *Sir Prianius* on 22 February 1957. The mixed rake of luggage vans, coaches and Pullmans must have taxed the 'King Arthur' to the full, yet it was on these boat trains that the famous engines had their last fling. [A. R. Butcher]

No.30786 *Sir Lionel* hurries through its home station, Eastleigh, with a Southampton-bound boat train, the 'Brittany Express', on 2 July 1954. [Brian Morrison]

The well-proportioned lines of a Maunsell 'King Arthur' are fully evident in this view of No. 30790 *Sir Villiars* at Weymouth on 8 June 1961. The high running-plates and long single splasher were inherited from Urie's drawing office, while the neat cab profile comes from Ashford. The doors between engine and tender were an LSWR feature of this design.
[M. Mensing]

No. 30773 *Sir Lavaine* blows off at 200lbs per sq.in. as it stands at the head of a stopper to Bournemouth in Weymouth station on 8 June 1959. The 'Arthurs' were excellent steamers and given reasonable maintenance would do everything required of them. The locomotive was massively built (80 tons) and the generous proportions of the frames and bearings stood the design in good stead during its long years of hard service.
[S. Rickard]

The last of the Knights of the Round Table, *Sir Prianius,* No.30770 stands in the evening sunlight at Eastleigh, polished up for hauling a society special, the 'South Western Limited', to Waterloo on 2 September 1962. As the engine was withdrawn two months later, the crisp beat of a 'King Arthur' in action could be heard no more on Southern metals and the Region never seemed quite the same without them. As reliable medium-powered express engines they had few faults and many qualities and have been remembered with affection by locomen and enthusiasts. [A. R. Butcher]

The 'S15' 4-6-0s were first cousins of the 'King Arthurs'. Like the express engines, they were developed by Maunsell from the Urie design, having the modern refinements of higher pressure and long travel valves. No.826 of Exmouth Junction, in its original condition without deflector plates eases around the Wilton curves with an up freight in the 1920's.
[L. T. George collection]

The original Urie version of the class; No.512 at Eastleigh in 1935. [L. T. George collection]

Fifteen 'S15's were built at Eastleigh in 1927, with a further series of ten (to be dealt with in a later volume) in 1936. No. 30828 went new to Salisbury and spent most of its working life at the shed. The engine looks in poor condition in this view at Eastleigh on 28 April 1963 and it was in fact withdrawn eight months later.

[D. M. Cox]

No.30828 in happier days. The engine is hard at work on the class of duty for which it was designed, the haulage of the heavy freight, 26 May 1960. The scene is Hewish summit, on the Salisbury–Exeter route, a line which saw 'S15's at work in considerable numbers from Salisbury and Exmouth Junction sheds.

[G. P. Brown]

The first of the Maunsell 'S15's, No.30823, has a quiet day out with the p.w. gang at Dinton, near Salisbury, on 12 June 1952. These mixed-traffic engines, with a tractive effort of 29,855lb, were classified 6F by British Railways. When first built they were painted lined-black, which although replaced by Maunsell green until the war years, gave rise to the engines' nickname of 'Black-uns'. [A. C. V. Kendall]

The graceful spire looming through the wintry mist proclaims the scene as Salisbury, with one of the local 'S15's, No. 30829, pulling away with a westbound goods in 1960. The start from Salisbury involved a steady uphill pull for some two miles westwards and these sure-footed 4-6-0s could heave heavy loads on their way with the minimum of fuss.
[G. A. Richardson]

Having 5ft 7in wheels, the 'S15's were excellent performers on stopping trains; No. 30831 of Salisbury (72B) pauses for passengers at Chard Junction on 4 May 1957. [A. E. Bennett]

The massive 5,000 gallon watercart is prominent in this photograph of No. 30823 on Yeovil shed, 2 June 1963. Some men claimed that these Urie tenders attached to the Nos. 30823–832 'S15's were more free-running than the Maunsell design provided for the later Nos. 30838–847 series. [D. M. Cox]

No.30823 in company with a variety of classes on Yeovil shed, 2 June 1963. Like most of Maunsell's larger engines, the 'S15's were fitted with smoke deflectors around 1930. Beneath the buffer beam can be seen the AWS equipment which was fitted in the early 1960's. [D. M. Cox]

In order to fit on the smaller Central Section turntables, Nos. 833–837 were fitted with six-wheeled 4,000 gallon Maunsell tenders in 1936. No. 30835 was operating from Redhill, along with Nos. 30836/7 in the mid-1950's, mainly working freights on the heavily graded cross-country line to Reading. The 4–6–0 is seen near Betchworth on 16 April 1956.
[A. R. Butcher]

No. 30834 (of Feltham), still with its six-wheeled tender, passes Woking with the 4.30 a.m. Eastleigh Feltham freight on 8 June 1964. The engine was withdrawn later in the same year. [P. J. Lync

109
30834
4

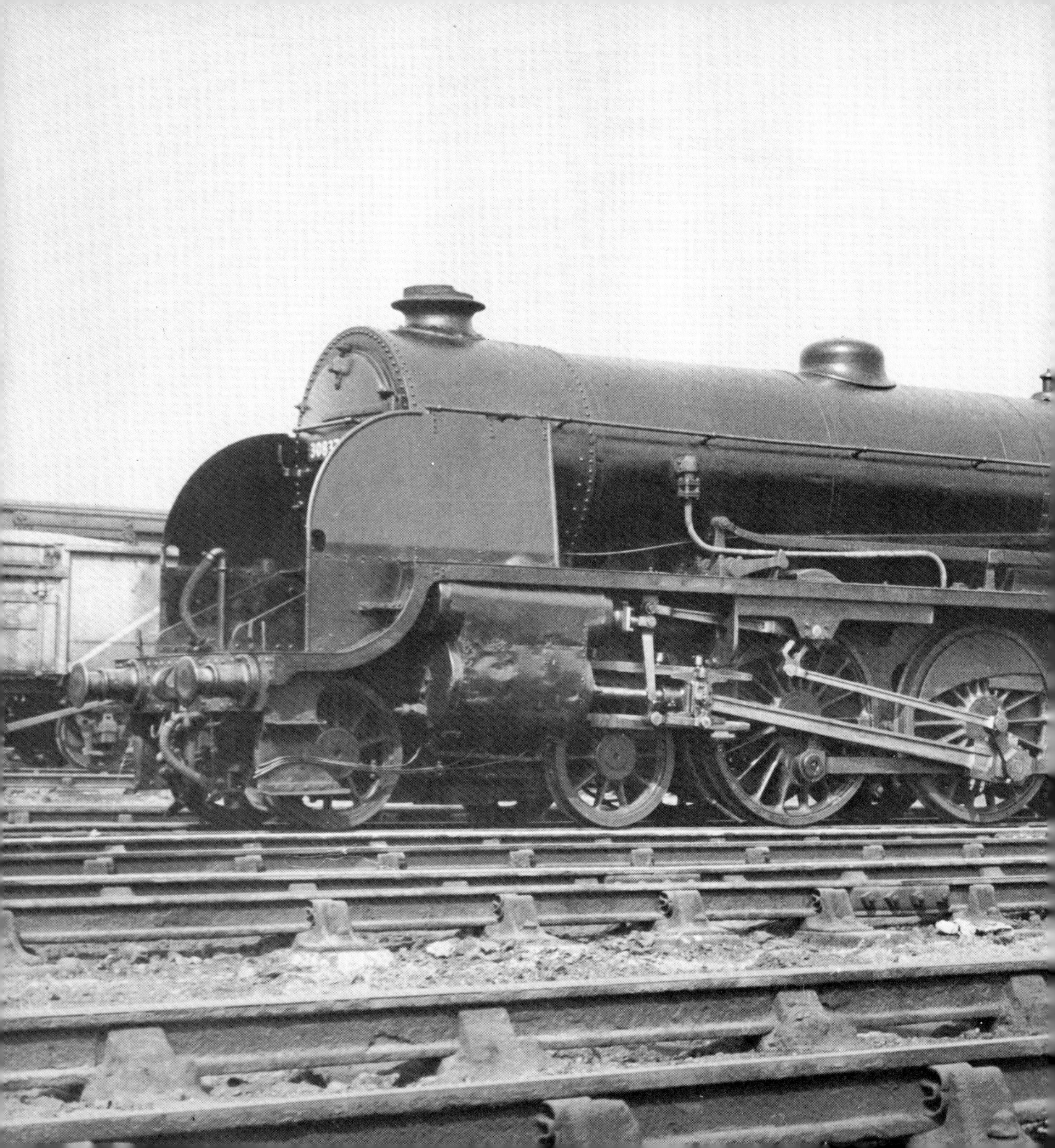

No. 30837, seen at Feltham on 1 May 1965, became the best-known member of the class, for it proved to be the last Maunsell 4-6-0 left in active service and in consequence was much in demand for special runs. For such turns it was generally kept in good external condition, and was the subject of many treasured photographs. The locomotive was one of two 'S15's which acquired 4,000 gallon tenders from scrapped 'Schools' 4-4-0s. This one was obtained from No. 30912 in June 1962.
[A. R. Butcher]

The Maunsell 'S15's could run up to 75mph when required and were often to be seen at work on heavy holiday reliefs in the summer months. No. 30825, then of Salisbury shed, hauls a heavy load through Vauxhall in August 1962.

[G. D. King]

A bleak winter contrast to the summer scenes pictured opposite. No.30831 clanks past snow-clad Semley, eighteen miles out from Salisbury, with a pick-up freight on 28 December 1962. The majority of railway photographs are taken on fine sunny days—but professional railwaymen have to put up with every facet of the English climate.

[G. A. Richardson]

These 5ft 7in 4-6-0s performed exceptionally well on the heavy gradients between Salisbury and Exeter, making good progress up the banks and, if in good fettle, racing downhill with tremendous zest. No.30829 emerges westbound from Honiton tunnel in 1962. [D. T. Cobbe]

30836
30053

The six-wheeled tender 'S15's put in a great deal of work on the Redhill-Reading line. No.30836, steaming well, starts out of Betchworth in the crisp spring sunshine, April 1963. Costing some £10,000 when built at Eastleigh in 1927, the 'S15's gave wonderful service for over 35 years, and must rank among the most successful of British mixed-traffic 4-6-0s. Like the 'King Arthurs' they were economical, light on maintenance and could be flogged when the need arose. [G. D. King]

o.30836, seen outside Eastleigh shed on 20 August 1960 has been into the Works for an intermediate verhaul—'soled and heeled'—and has had the smokebox only painted instead of a full repaint. [D. M. Cox]

o.30833 passes Clapham Junction with a Basingstoke train. This 'S15' was fitted with the tender from ithdrawn 'Schools' 4-4-0 No.30908 in 1962. [Stanley Creer]

The eight members of the 'Z' Class 0-8-0T were built at Brighton in 1929 for service as heavy-duty shunters in the largest marshalling yards. This view of No.30950, seen under repair at Eastleigh on 18 September 1960, shows the position of the inside (third) cylinder, which was served by its own set of Walschaerts valve gear between the frames. The use of three cylinders gave the engine a very even acceleration, and with 71 tons of locomotive on the eight-coupled wheels, there was a considerable freedom from slipping. [L. W. Rowe]

The boiler of the 'Z' Class was of standard Brighton design with large steam and water capacity, but small grate area, in order to store heat during periods of waiting and to minimise blowing off at the safety valves. The engine had no superheater, as it was considered an unnecessary complication on a shunting engine and likely to waste the steam when opening and shutting the regulator so often. No. 30955 still carried an Ashford (74A) shedplate on 16 April 1960 but it had been transferred with several companions to Exmouth Junction for banking duties between Exeter's St. Davids and Central stations.
[D. T. Cobbe]

A last look at a Maunsell machine in its heyday. 'King Arthur' No.456 *Sir Galahad* looks a credit to the cleaners at Salisbury shed as it hammers through Milborne Port, blowing off at 200lb per sq.in, with the first part of the down 'Atlantic Coast Express' on 22 August 1935. With excellent maintenance, plus skilled work from experienced footplatemen, these two-cylinder 4-6-0s of modest dimensions performed wonders on the fearsome gradients between Salisbury and Exeter, as well as on many other equally arduous routes, in the pre-War years. Although their work could not match the glamorous performance of the streamlined trains operating to the North of England, nevertheless for sheer consistency of running in everyday service their work could hardly be bettered anywhere in Britain. [L. T. George collection]